Moldova

Everything You Need to Know

Copyright © 2024 by Noah Gil-Smith.

All rights reserved. No part of this book may be reproduced, distributed, or transmitted in any form or by any means, including photocopying, recording, or other electronic or mechanical methods, without the prior written permission of the publisher, except in the case of brief quotations embodied in critical reviews and certain other noncommercial uses permitted by copyright law. This book was created with the assistance of Artificial Intelligence. The content presented in this book is for entertainment purposes only. It should not be considered as a substitute for professional advice or comprehensive research. Readers are encouraged to independently verify any information and consult relevant experts for specific matters. The author and publisher disclaim any liability or responsibility for any loss, injury, or inconvenience caused or alleged to be caused directly or indirectly by the information presented in this book.

Introduction to Moldova 6

The Geographic Landscape: A Closer Look at Moldova's Terrain 9

Moldova's Rich History: From Ancient Roots to Modern Times 11

The Birth of a Nation: Understanding Moldova's Independence 14

Moldova's Struggle for Identity: Navigating Through Historical Influences 17

Moldova's Cultural Mosaic: Traditions and Customs 20

Exploring Moldovan Cuisine: A Gastronomic Journey 23

Toasting with Țuică: Moldovan Beverages and Spirits 26

The Heartbeat of Moldova: Music and Dance Traditions 28

Moldovan Festivals and Celebrations: Embracing Local Spirit 30

Moldova's Literary Heritage: Words That Shape the Nation 33

Art and Craftsmanship in Moldova: Creativity Beyond Borders 36

Moldova's Wildlife Wonderland: Discovering Natural Treasures 39

The Moldovan Flora: A Botanical Delight 41

Moldova's Avian World: Birdwatching Bliss 43

Journey through Moldova's Historic Cities: Past Meets Present 45

Chisinau: The Vibrant Capital City 47

Tiraspol: Exploring Transnistria's Enigmatic Capital 49

Balti: Moldova's Northern Hub of Commerce and Culture 52

Cahul: A Southern Gem by the Prut River 54

Bender: A Tale of Fortresses and Crossroads 56

Soroca: The Gypsy Capital of Moldova 59

Orhei: A Journey to the Ancient Past 61

Gagauzia: Unveiling Moldova's Cultural Diversity 63

Moldova's Spiritual Heritage: Churches, Monasteries, and Synagogues 65

Moldova's Wine Legacy: Nectar of the Gods 67

Moldovan Wineries: Exploring the Wine Routes 70

Moldova's Soviet Legacy: Traces of a Bygone Era 72

Moldova's Independence Square: Symbol of National Sovereignty 75

Exploring Moldova's Archaeological Sites: Unearthing Ancient Treasures 77

The Moldovan Language: A Linguistic Journey 79

Moldovan Literature: Exploring National Voices 81

Moldova's Educational System: Nurturing Future Generations 84

Moldova's Healthcare System: Ensuring Well-being for All 87

Moldova's Economy: From Agriculture to Technology 90

Moldova's Political Landscape: A Democratic Journey 93

Moldova's European Integration: Navigating Toward the Future 96

Moldova's International Relations: Bridging East and West 99

Sustainable Development in Moldova: Preserving Nature and Heritage 102

Moldova's Transportation Network: Connecting Regions and Beyond 105

Exploring Moldova's Rural Life: Homestays and Agritourism 108

Moldova's Future: Opportunities and Challenges Ahead 111

Epilogue 114

Introduction to Moldova

Nestled in the heart of Eastern Europe lies a land steeped in history, culture, and natural beauty—Moldova. Bordered by Romania to the west and Ukraine to the north, east, and south, this enchanting country holds a rich tapestry of traditions and a resilient spirit that has withstood the test of time.

With a population of over 3.5 million people, Moldova is one of the smallest countries in Europe, yet its significance transcends its size. The capital city, Chisinau, serves as the bustling center of commerce, culture, and administration, while smaller towns and villages dot the countryside, each with its own unique charm and character.

Moldova's history is a testament to its resilience and endurance. Throughout the centuries, it has been a crossroads of civilizations, influenced by various cultures and empires. From the ancient Greeks and Romans to the Byzantines and Ottomans, Moldova's territory has been shaped by the ebb and flow of conquests and migrations.

One of the defining chapters in Moldova's history is its period under the principality of Moldavia, which flourished during the Middle Ages. This era saw the rise of powerful rulers such as Stephen the Great, who defended Moldova against Ottoman invasions and left behind a legacy of fortresses and monasteries that still stand today.

In the 19th century, Moldova came under Russian rule, and later became part of the Soviet Union after World War II. This period of Soviet domination left an indelible mark on Moldovan society, shaping its political, economic, and cultural landscape for decades to come.

Moldova gained independence from the Soviet Union in 1991, marking a new chapter in its history. Since then, the country has navigated its path toward democracy and economic development, facing numerous challenges along the way.

Today, Moldova stands at a crossroads, seeking to define its identity and forge its future in a rapidly changing world. While it grapples with issues such as corruption, poverty, and political instability, it also holds immense potential, with its fertile soil, burgeoning wine industry, and strategic location at the crossroads of Europe and Asia.

But Moldova is more than just its history and challenges—it is a land of breathtaking landscapes, from rolling hills and vineyards to lush forests and winding rivers. Its people are known for their warmth, hospitality, and resilience, embodying the spirit of a nation that has overcome adversity time and time again.

As we embark on this journey to discover Moldova, let us delve deeper into its history, culture, and natural beauty, and uncover the hidden gems that make this country truly unique. From its ancient fortresses to its bustling markets, from its traditional cuisine to its vibrant festivals, Moldova beckons us to explore its wonders and uncover its secrets. So come along and join me as we embark on an unforgettable adventure through the heart of Eastern Europe—to the land of Moldova.

The Geographic Landscape: A Closer Look at Moldova's Terrain

Moldova, nestled in the southeastern corner of Europe, boasts a diverse and captivating geographic landscape. Despite being one of the smallest countries on the continent, Moldova's terrain is rich and varied, offering a blend of fertile plains, rolling hills, and picturesque rivers.

At the heart of Moldova lies the vast Moldavian Plateau, a gently undulating expanse that covers much of the country's central and eastern regions. Characterized by its fertile soils and mild climate, the plateau is an agricultural heartland, supporting the cultivation of crops such as wheat, corn, sunflowers, and grapes—the backbone of Moldova's renowned wine industry.

To the north, the landscape gives way to the Codrii Forest, a dense and ancient woodland that stretches along the border with Ukraine. Home to a rich diversity of flora and fauna, including oak, beech, and pine trees, as well as deer, boar, and numerous bird species, the Codrii Forest is a haven for nature lovers and outdoor enthusiasts.

In the south, the terrain becomes more rugged as it approaches the foothills of the Carpathian Mountains, which form Moldova's western border with Romania. Here, the landscape is punctuated by deep river valleys and rocky outcrops, offering stunning vistas and opportunities for hiking, camping, and adventure.

Moldova is also crisscrossed by a network of rivers, the most significant of which is the Dniester, which flows from north to south through the heart of the country. The Dniester River not only provides a vital source of water for agriculture and industry but also serves as a natural boundary, separating Moldova from the breakaway region of Transnistria to the east.

To the west, the Prut River marks Moldova's border with Romania, meandering through fertile valleys and past quaint villages before joining the Danube and flowing into the Black Sea. The Prut River Valley is known for its scenic beauty and cultural heritage, with historic towns such as Cahul and Ungheni dotted along its banks.

Overall, Moldova's geographic landscape is a harmonious blend of fertile plains, verdant forests, and meandering rivers, offering a wealth of natural beauty and recreational opportunities for residents and visitors alike. From the lush vineyards of the central plateau to the rugged beauty of the Carpathian foothills, Moldova's terrain is as diverse as it is enchanting, inviting exploration and discovery at every turn.

Moldova's Rich History: From Ancient Roots to Modern Times

Moldova's rich history is a tapestry woven from ancient roots to modern times, reflecting a diverse array of cultures, civilizations, and influences that have shaped the land and its people over millennia. The story of Moldova begins in antiquity, with evidence of human habitation dating back thousands of years. Archaeological discoveries have unearthed traces of Neolithic settlements, Bronze Age artifacts, and ancient fortifications, attesting to the region's significance as a crossroads of civilizations.

In the classical era, Moldova's territory was inhabited by various tribes and peoples, including the Thracians, Scythians, and Dacians, who left behind a legacy of myths, legends, and archaeological wonders. The Dacian fortress of Dava, located near present-day Orhei, stands as a testament to their advanced civilization and military prowess.

During the Roman period, Moldova was part of the province of Dacia, a frontier region on the northeastern edge of the empire. Roman legions built roads, fortresses, and settlements throughout the territory, leaving a lasting impact on the landscape and culture of the region.

In the Middle Ages, Moldova emerged as a distinct political entity under the principality of Moldavia, which was founded in the 14th century by a mix of local and foreign rulers. The reign of Stephen the Great, who ruled from 1457 to 1504, is considered a golden age in Moldovan history, marked by military victories against the Ottoman Empire and the construction of numerous churches, monasteries, and fortresses.

In the 16th century, Moldova came under Ottoman rule, becoming a vassal state of the Ottoman Empire for several centuries. Despite this period of foreign domination, Moldova retained a degree of autonomy and continued to develop its culture, language, and identity.

In the 19th century, Moldova experienced a series of territorial changes and political upheavals, as it came under Russian influence and later became part of the Russian Empire. The Treaty of Paris in 1856 saw Moldova united with Wallachia to form the Principality of Romania, laying the groundwork for the modern Romanian state.

Following the collapse of the Russian Empire in the aftermath of World War I, Moldova became part of Greater Romania, a period characterized by economic development, cultural revival, and territorial expansion. However, this era was short-lived, as Moldova was annexed by the Soviet Union in 1940 as a result of the Molotov-Ribbentrop Pact.

During World War II, Moldova suffered significant devastation and loss of life, as it became a battleground between Axis and Soviet forces. After the war, Moldova was incorporated into the Soviet Union as the Moldavian Soviet Socialist Republic, undergoing a period of industrialization, collectivization, and Russification.

Moldova gained independence from the Soviet Union in 1991, following the collapse of communism in Eastern Europe. Since then, the country has faced numerous challenges, including political instability, economic hardship, and territorial disputes. Today, Moldova is striving to build a democratic society, promote economic development, and strengthen its ties with the European Union and the international community.

From its ancient origins to its modern struggles and triumphs, Moldova's history is a testament to the resilience, endurance, and spirit of its people. As the country continues to navigate its path toward the future, it remains grounded in its rich cultural heritage and historical legacy, embracing the complexities of its past while striving to shape a brighter tomorrow.

The Birth of a Nation: Understanding Moldova's Independence

The birth of Moldova as an independent nation is a chapter in history that reflects the tumultuous changes that swept across Eastern Europe in the late 20th century. Moldova's journey to independence was marked by political upheaval, social unrest, and the collapse of the Soviet Union.

In the late 1980s and early 1990s, as the winds of change swept through the Soviet bloc, calls for greater autonomy and independence began to echo across Moldova. The region's long-standing grievances, rooted in historical injustices and ethnic tensions, simmered beneath the surface, fueling demands for self-determination and sovereignty.

In August 1991, following the failed coup attempt in Moscow and the subsequent dissolution of the Soviet Union, Moldova seized the opportunity to assert its independence. On August 27, 1991, the Moldovan parliament declared the country's independence from the Soviet Union, adopting a declaration of sovereignty and national symbols, including the tricolor flag and the coat of arms.

However, Moldova's path to independence was fraught with challenges and obstacles. The country's multi-ethnic makeup, with significant Russian, Ukrainian, and Gagauz minorities, posed complex issues of identity and allegiance. In particular, the breakaway region of Transnistria, populated largely by ethnic Russians and Ukrainians, declared its independence from Moldova in September 1990, sparking a protracted conflict that would last for years.

The Transnistrian War, which erupted in 1992, pitted Moldovan forces against Transnistrian separatists backed by Russian troops, resulting in a devastating conflict that claimed thousands of lives and displaced hundreds of thousands of people. Despite efforts to broker a ceasefire and negotiate a peaceful resolution, the conflict remains unresolved to this day, casting a shadow over Moldova's quest for stability and unity.

In the aftermath of independence, Moldova faced numerous challenges as it sought to build a democratic society, promote economic development, and establish its place on the world stage. The transition from a centrally planned economy to a market-oriented system was fraught with difficulties, leading to widespread poverty, unemployment, and social unrest.

Political instability and corruption further hampered Moldova's progress, undermining public trust in the government and impeding efforts to enact meaningful reforms. Despite these challenges, Moldova made strides toward democratization and European integration, joining the Council of Europe in 1995 and signing an Association Agreement with the European Union in 2014.

Today, Moldova continues to grapple with the legacy of its past and the challenges of its present, as it strives to overcome divisions, promote reconciliation, and build a brighter future for its people. The journey toward independence may have been fraught with obstacles, but it also symbolizes the resilience, determination, and aspirations of a nation striving to carve out its place in the world.

Moldova's Struggle for Identity: Navigating Through Historical Influences

Moldova's struggle for identity is a nuanced tale of navigating through the historical influences that have shaped the nation's cultural landscape. Situated at the crossroads of Europe and Asia, Moldova's identity is a mosaic of diverse ethnic, linguistic, and religious traditions that reflect its complex history of conquests, migrations, and interactions with neighboring peoples and empires.

One of the defining features of Moldova's identity is its linguistic diversity, with both Romanian and Russian serving as official languages. Romanian, the native tongue of the majority of Moldova's population, is closely related to other Romance languages and serves as a symbol of Moldova's cultural ties to neighboring Romania. Russian, meanwhile, is spoken by a significant minority of Moldova's population, particularly in urban areas and regions with large Russian-speaking communities.

Religion has also played a central role in shaping Moldova's identity, with Orthodox Christianity serving as the predominant faith. The Moldovan

Orthodox Church, an autocephalous branch of the Eastern Orthodox Church, traces its roots back to the medieval principality of Moldavia and remains a key institution in Moldovan society, providing spiritual guidance and moral support to millions of believers.

Historically, Moldova's territory has been subject to numerous foreign influences, including Byzantine, Ottoman, and Russian rule, each leaving its mark on the region's culture, architecture, and traditions. The legacy of these empires is evident in Moldova's culinary customs, artistic heritage, and religious practices, which reflect a blend of Eastern and Western influences.

In the 20th century, Moldova's struggle for identity was further complicated by its status as a constituent republic of the Soviet Union. Under Soviet rule, Moldova underwent a process of Russification, with the imposition of Russian language and culture and the suppression of Moldovan national identity. However, despite these efforts to assimilate Moldova into the Soviet mold, the country's cultural heritage remained resilient, preserved through folk traditions, literature, and music.

Since gaining independence in 1991, Moldova has grappled with the challenges of nation-building and forging a cohesive national identity. Efforts to promote Moldovan language and culture, celebrate national holidays and symbols, and commemorate historical figures have been met with varying degrees of success, as Moldova continues to navigate the complexities of its multicultural heritage.

In recent years, Moldova's struggle for identity has been further complicated by geopolitical tensions and regional divisions, particularly in the breakaway region of Transnistria. The unresolved conflict in Transnistria, along with competing claims to Moldova's historical legacy by neighboring countries, has underscored the fragile nature of Moldova's identity and the need for greater unity and solidarity among its people.

Despite these challenges, Moldova's struggle for identity is an ongoing process, shaped by the country's past, present, and future aspirations. As Moldova seeks to define itself in the 21st century, it draws upon its rich cultural heritage, linguistic diversity, and historical legacy to forge a path forward that is rooted in unity, inclusivity, and respect for its multicultural identity.

Moldova's Cultural Mosaic: Traditions and Customs

Moldova's cultural mosaic is a vibrant tapestry woven from a rich tapestry of traditions and customs that reflect the country's diverse ethnic, religious, and historical heritage. From folk music and dance to culinary delights and religious celebrations, Moldova's cultural landscape is as diverse as it is captivating.

One of the most enduring traditions in Moldova is the celebration of Easter, a cherished holiday that holds deep religious significance for the majority Orthodox Christian population. Easter in Moldova is a time of joyous feasting, religious processions, and elaborate egg decorating rituals, known as "pisanie." Families gather to attend church services, share traditional dishes such as cozonac (sweet bread) and pasca (Easter cake), and exchange brightly colored eggs as symbols of rebirth and renewal.

Another hallmark of Moldovan culture is its rich musical heritage, which encompasses a wide range of genres, from traditional folk songs to classical symphonies. Moldovan folk music is characterized by its haunting melodies, intricate vocal harmonies, and lively dance rhythms, often accompanied by traditional instruments such as the cobza, accordion, and flute. Dance is also an integral part of Moldovan culture, with traditional dances such as the hora and the sirba performed at weddings, festivals, and other special occasions.

Moldova's culinary traditions are a testament to the country's agrarian heritage and its fertile soil, which yields an abundance of fruits, vegetables, grains, and wine grapes. Traditional Moldovan cuisine is hearty, flavorful, and influenced by a mix of Romanian, Russian, Ukrainian, and Turkish culinary traditions. Staple dishes include mamaliga (cornmeal porridge), sarmale (stuffed cabbage rolls), placinta (stuffed pastry), and various types of pickled vegetables and preserves. Wine is also a central element of Moldovan gastronomy, with the country's vineyards producing a wide variety of high-quality wines, including the famous Moldovan reds and whites.

Moldova's cultural calendar is dotted with numerous festivals, fairs, and celebrations that showcase the country's rich heritage and traditions. One such event is Martisor, a spring festival celebrated on March 1st, during which people exchange small tokens of good luck and prosperity, typically in the form of red and white tassels. Other notable festivals include Dragobete, a celebration of love and fertility held in February, and Mărțișor, a celebration of women and the coming of spring.

Religious customs and rituals also play a significant role in Moldovan culture, with Orthodox Christian holidays such as Christmas and Epiphany observed with reverence and solemnity. Religious icons, crosses, and shrines adorn many Moldovan homes and public spaces, serving as symbols of faith and devotion.

Overall, Moldova's cultural mosaic is a testament to the country's rich and diverse heritage, shaped by centuries of history, tradition, and innovation. From its colorful festivals and musical traditions to its hearty cuisine and religious customs, Moldova's cultural tapestry is a source of pride and inspiration for its people, embodying the spirit of resilience, creativity, and community that defines this unique corner of Eastern Europe.

Exploring Moldovan Cuisine: A Gastronomic Journey

Embark on a gastronomic journey through Moldova, where every dish tells a story of tradition, culture, and culinary creativity. Moldovan cuisine is a delightful fusion of flavors, drawing influence from Romanian, Russian, Ukrainian, and Turkish culinary traditions. At the heart of Moldovan cooking lies a reverence for fresh, seasonal ingredients and a love for hearty, comforting dishes that nourish both body and soul.

One of the staples of Moldovan cuisine is mamaliga, a traditional cornmeal porridge that serves as the cornerstone of many meals. Similar to Italian polenta or Romanian mămăligă, mamaliga is often served as a side dish alongside meat, cheese, or vegetables, or topped with sour cream or melted butter for added richness.

Another beloved dish in Moldovan cuisine is sarmale, or stuffed cabbage rolls, which are typically filled with a savory mixture of ground meat, rice, onions, and spices, then simmered in a flavorful tomato sauce until tender and fragrant. Sarmale are a staple of festive occasions such as weddings, holidays, and family gatherings, where they are served alongside other traditional dishes such as placinta (stuffed pastry), pickled vegetables, and various types of cured meats and cheeses.

No exploration of Moldovan cuisine would be complete without sampling the country's famous wines, which are celebrated for their exceptional quality and diversity. Moldova boasts one of the oldest and most prolific wine industries in the world, with vineyards stretching across the picturesque countryside and producing a wide variety of reds, whites, and sparkling wines. From the robust reds of Purcari to the crisp whites of Cricova, Moldovan wines offer something for every palate and occasion.

In addition to mamaliga and sarmale, Moldovan cuisine features a wealth of other traditional dishes that reflect the country's agrarian heritage and culinary ingenuity. Placinta, a type of stuffed pastry, comes in many variations, including sweet and savory fillings such as cheese, cabbage, pumpkin, or apples. Pickled vegetables, known as muraturi, are a popular accompaniment to many meals, providing a tangy contrast to the rich flavors of meat and dairy dishes.

For those with a sweet tooth, Moldovan cuisine offers an array of delectable desserts and pastries that showcase the country's love for all things sweet. Pasca, a traditional Easter cake made with sweetened cheese and raisins, is a favorite treat during the holiday season, while cozonac, a sweet bread enriched with eggs, butter, and sugar, is enjoyed year-round as a special indulgence.

Overall, exploring Moldovan cuisine is a journey of discovery and delight, where every bite offers a taste of the country's rich cultural heritage and culinary traditions. Whether savoring a steaming bowl of mamaliga, indulging in a plate of sarmale, or raising a glass of fine Moldovan wine, the flavors of Moldova are sure to leave a lasting impression on your taste buds and your heart.

Toasting with Țuică: Moldovan Beverages and Spirits

When it comes to Moldovan beverages and spirits, one cannot overlook the iconic țuică, a traditional fruit brandy that holds a special place in the hearts and glasses of Moldovans. Made from fermented fruits such as plums, apples, or grapes, țuică is a beloved staple of Moldovan culture, enjoyed on festive occasions, family gatherings, and social gatherings alike.

The process of making țuică is a labor of love that begins with the careful selection of ripe, high-quality fruits, which are then crushed, fermented, and distilled to produce a potent and aromatic spirit. Each region of Moldova has its own unique variations of țuică, with different fruits, distillation methods, and aging techniques yielding distinct flavors and characteristics.

In addition to țuică, Moldova is also renowned for its wine production, which dates back thousands of years to ancient times. Moldova boasts one of the oldest and most prolific wine industries in the world, with vineyards covering over 112,000 hectares of land and producing a diverse array of red, white, and sparkling wines.

One of the most famous wine regions in Moldova is the Codru wine region, located in the central part of the country. Here, fertile soils, a temperate climate, and a long tradition of winemaking combine to produce some of Moldova's finest wines, including robust reds such as Fetească Neagră and elegant whites such as Fetească Albă.

Another notable wine region in Moldova is the Purcari wine region, located in the south-eastern part of the country near the border with Ukraine. Purcari is renowned for its rich, full-bodied red wines, particularly its eponymous Purcari blend, which has won numerous awards and accolades on the international stage.

In addition to wine and țuică, Moldova also produces a variety of other alcoholic beverages, including beer, vodka, and liqueurs. Moldovan beer is characterized by its crisp, refreshing taste and is enjoyed by locals and visitors alike, particularly during the hot summer months. Moldovan vodka, known as horincă, is a strong and fiery spirit made from grains or potatoes and is often enjoyed as a shot or mixed into cocktails.

Overall, Moldova's beverages and spirits reflect the country's rich cultural heritage, agricultural abundance, and passion for craftsmanship and tradition. Whether raising a glass of țuică in celebration, sipping on a glass of fine Moldovan wine, or enjoying a cold beer with friends, the flavors of Moldova are sure to delight and inspire all who partake.

The Heartbeat of Moldova: Music and Dance Traditions

In Moldova, music and dance are more than just forms of entertainment—they are the heartbeat of the nation, pulsing with the rhythms of tradition, culture, and community. Moldovan music and dance traditions are as diverse as the country's landscape, reflecting influences from Romania, Russia, Ukraine, and beyond.

At the heart of Moldovan musical culture is folk music, which encompasses a wide range of genres and styles, from lively dance tunes to soulful ballads. Traditional Moldovan folk music is characterized by its haunting melodies, intricate vocal harmonies, and lively rhythms, often accompanied by instruments such as the cobza (a type of lute), accordion, and flute.

One of the most beloved forms of Moldovan folk music is the hora, a traditional circle dance that is performed at weddings, festivals, and other special occasions. The hora is a joyful celebration of community and camaraderie, with dancers joining hands and moving in a circular pattern to the lively rhythms of traditional Moldovan music.

Another popular Moldovan dance tradition is the sirba, a fast-paced dance characterized by quick footwork and intricate patterns. The sirba is often accompanied by lively instrumental music, featuring instruments such as the violin, accordion, and clarinet, and is a favorite among dancers of all ages.

In addition to folk music and dance, Moldova also has a rich tradition of classical music, with composers such as Eugen Doga, Mihail Glinka, and Ciprian Porumbescu making significant contributions to the genre. Moldovan classical music is celebrated for its elegance, sophistication, and emotional depth, with orchestral compositions, operas, and chamber music pieces that reflect the country's cultural heritage and artistic excellence.

In recent years, Moldova has also embraced modern music genres such as pop, rock, and hip-hop, with a burgeoning music scene that is gaining recognition both domestically and internationally. Moldovan musicians and bands are making waves on the global stage, with their unique blend of traditional influences and contemporary sensibilities captivating audiences around the world.

Overall, music and dance are integral parts of Moldovan culture, serving as expressions of identity, community, and creativity. Whether performing a traditional hora at a wedding, attending a classical concert in Chisinau, or dancing the night away at a local club, the music and rhythms of Moldova are sure to leave a lasting impression on all who experience them.

Moldovan Festivals and Celebrations: Embracing Local Spirit

Moldova's festivals and celebrations are a vibrant tapestry of traditions, rituals, and community spirit that reflect the rich cultural heritage of the nation. Throughout the year, Moldovans gather to celebrate a diverse array of holidays, festivals, and special occasions that mark the passage of time and honor the country's customs and traditions.

One of the most beloved festivals in Moldova is Martisor, celebrated on March 1st, which marks the beginning of spring. Martisor is a time of renewal and rebirth, when people exchange small tokens of good luck and prosperity, typically in the form of red and white tassels. These Martisor trinkets are worn as symbols of hope and anticipation for the arrival of warmer weather and brighter days ahead.

Another important holiday in Moldova is Easter, a deeply religious observance that holds special significance for the majority Orthodox Christian population. Easter in Moldova is a time of joyous celebration, marked by church services, family gatherings, and elaborate feasts. Traditional dishes such as cozonac (sweet bread), pasca (Easter cake), and colored eggs are enjoyed, while religious processions and rituals symbolize the resurrection of Jesus Christ and the promise of eternal life.

In addition to religious holidays, Moldova also celebrates a number of secular festivals and events that highlight the country's cultural heritage and traditions. One such event is the National Wine Day, held annually in October, which pays homage to Moldova's rich winemaking heritage. During the festival, vineyards and wineries across the country open their doors to visitors, offering tastings, tours, and entertainment.

Moldova also celebrates a number of traditional folk festivals throughout the year, which showcase the country's vibrant music, dance, and craft traditions. One such festival is the Mărțișor, held in February, which celebrates the coming of spring and honors women. During Mărțișor, people exchange small trinkets and gifts, attend folk performances, and participate in various cultural activities.

Throughout the summer months, Moldova comes alive with music festivals, food fairs, and outdoor concerts that draw visitors from near and far. One of the most popular music festivals is the Gugutse International Festival, which showcases traditional Moldovan music and dance, as well as performances by artists from around the world.

Overall, Moldova's festivals and celebrations are a testament to the country's vibrant cultural scene and strong sense of community. Whether celebrating religious holidays, cultural traditions, or the joys of spring and summer, Moldovans come together to embrace their local spirit and celebrate life's blessings with warmth, hospitality, and joy.

Moldova's Literary Heritage: Words That Shape the Nation

Moldova's literary heritage is a testament to the power of words to shape a nation's identity, culture, and history. From ancient epics and folklore to modern novels and poetry, Moldovan literature reflects the rich tapestry of the country's cultural heritage and the diverse influences that have shaped its literary tradition.

One of the oldest and most enduring forms of Moldovan literature is folk poetry, which has been passed down through generations in the form of oral ballads, songs, and legends. These folk poems, known as "doinas" or "cântece populare," capture the essence of Moldovan life, celebrating love, nature, and the human spirit with lyrical beauty and timeless wisdom.

In addition to folk poetry, Moldova has a rich tradition of epic poetry, with epic tales such as "Miorița" and "Sadoveanu's Răzvan and Vidra" recounting heroic deeds, tragic love stories, and moral lessons that resonate with audiences to this day. These epic poems, often recited at weddings, funerals, and other important events, serve as a source of inspiration and cultural pride for Moldovans.

During the 19th and early 20th centuries, Moldovan literature underwent a period of rapid growth and development, fueled by a newfound sense of national identity and the rise of Romanian nationalism. Writers such as Alecu Russo, Alexandru Hâjdeu, and Mihai Eminescu played key roles in shaping Moldova's literary landscape, producing works that celebrated the country's language, culture, and history.

In the Soviet era, Moldovan literature experienced both censorship and promotion, as the communist regime sought to control and manipulate cultural expression for its own ideological purposes. Writers such as Grigore Vieru and Ion Druță emerged as prominent figures in Moldovan literature during this period, producing works that explored themes of social justice, national identity, and the human condition.

Since gaining independence in 1991, Moldova's literary scene has continued to evolve and diversify, with writers exploring new genres, themes, and styles in response to the changing political, social, and cultural landscape. Contemporary Moldovan literature encompasses a wide range of voices and perspectives, from traditionalists who celebrate the country's cultural heritage to avant-garde writers who push the boundaries of artistic expression.

Today, Moldova's literary heritage is celebrated and preserved through a variety of cultural institutions, including libraries, museums, and literary festivals. Writers such as Dumitru Matcovschi, Natalia Barbu, and Nicolae Dabija continue to enrich Moldova's literary tradition with their unique voices and perspectives, ensuring that the country's literary heritage remains vibrant and relevant for generations to come.

Art and Craftsmanship in Moldova: Creativity Beyond Borders

Art and craftsmanship in Moldova are vibrant expressions of the country's rich cultural heritage and creative spirit. From traditional crafts such as pottery and weaving to contemporary art forms such as painting and sculpture, Moldovan artists and artisans continue to push the boundaries of creativity and innovation, drawing inspiration from their surroundings, their history, and their imagination.

One of the most enduring traditions in Moldovan craftsmanship is pottery, which has been practiced for centuries by skilled artisans who use locally sourced clay to create functional and decorative vessels. Moldovan pottery is known for its intricate designs, vibrant colors, and distinctive shapes, with each piece reflecting the unique style and personality of its creator.

In addition to pottery, Moldova is also renowned for its traditional weaving and embroidery techniques, which have been passed down through generations of artisans. Moldovan textiles are characterized by their intricate patterns, bright colors, and fine craftsmanship, with techniques such as cross-stitch, beadwork, and appliqué used to create stunning works of art that adorn clothing, home décor, and ceremonial objects.

Moldovan artists have also made significant contributions to the fields of painting, sculpture, and visual arts, with many gaining recognition both domestically and internationally for their talent and creativity. The Chisinau National Art Museum, founded in 1939, houses an impressive collection of Moldovan and international art, including paintings, sculptures, and decorative arts that span centuries of artistic expression.

Contemporary art galleries and studios in Moldova's capital city of Chisinau showcase the work of emerging and established artists working in a variety of mediums, from traditional oil painting and sculpture to multimedia installations and performance art. These spaces provide a platform for artists to share their vision, engage with the public, and contribute to the cultural life of the country.

In recent years, Moldova has also seen a resurgence of interest in traditional crafts and folk art, with organizations and initiatives working to preserve and promote these important cultural traditions. Craft fairs, workshops, and festivals celebrating pottery, weaving, embroidery, and other crafts are held regularly throughout the country, providing opportunities for artisans to showcase their work, exchange ideas, and connect with buyers and collectors.

Overall, art and craftsmanship in Moldova are thriving expressions of the country's cultural identity and creative energy. Whether practicing time-honored traditions or exploring new forms of artistic expression, Moldovan artists and artisans continue to inspire, innovate, and enrich the cultural landscape of their country and beyond.

Moldova's Wildlife Wonderland: Discovering Natural Treasures

Moldova's wildlife wonderland is a hidden gem waiting to be discovered, offering a diverse array of natural treasures and breathtaking landscapes. Despite its small size, Moldova boasts a surprising variety of habitats, including forests, wetlands, and grasslands, that provide a home to a rich and diverse array of plant and animal species.

One of the most iconic animals in Moldova is the European bison, also known as the wisent, which is native to the region and can be found in protected areas such as Codru Reserve and Râșcani Forest. These majestic creatures, which were once on the brink of extinction, have made a remarkable comeback in recent years thanks to conservation efforts aimed at protecting their habitat and reintroducing them into the wild.

In addition to European bison, Moldova is also home to a variety of other mammal species, including deer, wild boar, foxes, and wolves. These animals can often be spotted in the country's forests and woodlands, where they roam freely in search of food and shelter.

Birdwatchers will also find plenty to see in Moldova, with over 300 species of birds recorded in the country, including migratory birds such as storks, cranes, and swallows. The Prut and

Dniester rivers, as well as the Danube Delta Biosphere Reserve, provide important breeding and nesting grounds for many bird species, making them popular destinations for birdwatching enthusiasts.

Moldova's wetlands and marshes are also teeming with life, providing vital habitat for a variety of amphibians, reptiles, and aquatic species. The Lower Prut Nature Reserve, located along the banks of the Prut River, is home to numerous species of fish, frogs, and turtles, as well as rare and endangered plants that thrive in the region's unique wetland ecosystem.

In addition to its natural beauty, Moldova also boasts several protected areas and nature reserves that are dedicated to preserving the country's wildlife and ecosystems. These include Codru Reserve, Râșcani Forest, and Padurea Domnească Natural Park, which offer visitors the chance to explore pristine forests, meadows, and wetlands while observing native flora and fauna in their natural habitats.

Overall, Moldova's wildlife wonderland is a testament to the country's commitment to conservation and environmental stewardship. Whether exploring its forests, wetlands, or grasslands, visitors to Moldova are sure to be enchanted by the natural beauty and biodiversity that abound in this charming Eastern European country.

The Moldovan Flora: A Botanical Delight

The Moldovan flora is a botanical delight, boasting a rich tapestry of plant species that thrive in the country's diverse landscapes and climates. From the lush forests of Codru to the sun-drenched vineyards of Purcari, Moldova's flora is as varied as it is beautiful, with thousands of plant species that contribute to the country's natural beauty and biodiversity.

One of the most iconic plants in Moldova is the grapevine, which has been cultivated in the region for thousands of years and plays a central role in the country's agricultural economy and cultural heritage. Moldova is one of the largest wine-producing countries in the world, with vineyards covering over 112,000 hectares of land and producing a wide variety of red, white, and sparkling wines.

In addition to grapes, Moldova is also home to a diverse array of wildflowers, herbs, and medicinal plants that grow in the country's forests, meadows, and wetlands. Wildflowers such as daisies, poppies, and buttercups paint the countryside with bursts of color, while herbs such as chamomile, mint, and thyme are prized for their culinary and medicinal properties.

Moldova's forests are home to a variety of tree species, including oak, beech, pine, and hornbeam, which provide important habitat for wildlife and help to regulate the climate and water cycle. The Codru Reserve, located in central Moldova, is one of the largest and oldest protected forests in the country, with over 40,000 hectares of pristine woodland that is home to rare and endangered plant species.

Wetlands and marshes also play a crucial role in Moldova's ecosystem, providing habitat for a variety of aquatic plants such as reeds, cattails, and water lilies, as well as migratory birds and other wildlife. The Danube Delta Biosphere Reserve, located in southern Moldova, is one of the largest wetland ecosystems in Europe, with over 4,000 species of plants and animals that thrive in its labyrinth of waterways, lakes, and marshes.

Overall, the Moldovan flora is a testament to the country's natural beauty and ecological richness. Whether exploring its forests, vineyards, or wetlands, visitors to Moldova are sure to be captivated by the botanical diversity and splendor that abound in this enchanting corner of Eastern Europe.

Moldova's Avian World: Birdwatching Bliss

Moldova's avian world is a birdwatcher's paradise, offering enthusiasts the opportunity to observe a diverse array of bird species in their natural habitats. With over 300 species of birds recorded in the country, Moldova boasts a rich and varied avifauna that includes both resident and migratory species.

One of the most iconic birds in Moldova is the stork, which is revered as a symbol of good luck and prosperity. Storks can be found nesting on rooftops, chimneys, and utility poles throughout the country, particularly in rural areas where they build their massive nests and raise their young. Each spring, thousands of storks migrate to Moldova from their wintering grounds in Africa, filling the skies with their distinctive calls and graceful flight.

In addition to storks, Moldova is also home to a variety of other migratory birds, including cranes, swallows, and warblers, which pass through the country on their annual migrations between Europe, Asia, and Africa. The Prut and Dniester rivers, as well as the Danube Delta Biosphere Reserve, provide important breeding and nesting grounds for many bird species, making them popular destinations for birdwatching enthusiasts.

Birdwatching in Moldova is a year-round activity, with different seasons offering unique opportunities to observe different species of birds. In the spring, migrants such as hoopoes, bee-eaters, and nightingales arrive in Moldova to breed, filling the countryside with their vibrant colors and melodious songs. In the summer, wetlands and marshes come alive with the sights and sounds of waterfowl such as herons, egrets, and ducks, while in the fall, migratory birds such as geese and cranes pass through on their way to warmer climates.

One of the best places to go birdwatching in Moldova is the Lower Prut Nature Reserve, located along the banks of the Prut River, which is home to a variety of bird species as well as other wildlife such as mammals, reptiles, and amphibians. Other popular birdwatching destinations include the Padurea Domnească Natural Park, the Codru Reserve, and the Transnistria region, which is known for its diverse avifauna and unique habitats.

Overall, Moldova's avian world is a treasure trove of biodiversity and natural beauty, offering birdwatching enthusiasts the chance to observe and appreciate the rich diversity of bird life that thrives in this charming Eastern European country. Whether exploring wetlands, woodlands, or riverbanks, visitors to Moldova are sure to be captivated by the sights and sounds of its feathered inhabitants.

Journey through Moldova's Historic Cities: Past Meets Present

Embark on a captivating journey through Moldova's historic cities, where the echoes of the past mingle with the rhythms of modern life. Each city in Moldova tells its own unique story, weaving together layers of history, culture, and architecture that span centuries of human civilization.

Chisinau, the capital city of Moldova, is a vibrant metropolis that serves as the cultural, political, and economic heart of the country. Founded in the 15th century, Chisinau has undergone numerous transformations over the years, from a small market town to a bustling urban center with a rich architectural heritage. Visitors to Chisinau can explore its historic landmarks such as the Nativity Cathedral, Triumphal Arch, and Stefan cel Mare Central Park, as well as its lively markets, cafes, and cultural institutions.

Another gem in Moldova's crown is Orhei, a picturesque city located on the banks of the Raut River in central Moldova. Orhei is renowned for its stunning natural beauty, with rolling hills, lush vineyards, and dramatic limestone cliffs that overlook the river valley. The city is also home to several important archaeological sites, including the Orheiul Vechi Monastery Complex, which dates back to the 13th century and is considered one of the most important cultural and religious sites in Moldova. Balti, located in northern Moldova, is the country's second-largest city and a major industrial and commercial center. Founded in the 15th century, Balti has a rich history that is reflected in its diverse architectural styles, from Soviet-era apartment blocks to elegant 19th-century mansions. The city is also known for its vibrant cultural scene, with theaters, museums, and galleries that showcase the talents of local artists and performers.

Tiraspol, the capital of the breakaway region of Transnistria, is a city that is steeped in history and political intrigue. Founded in the 18th century by Russian settlers, Tiraspol has a unique character and identity that sets it apart from the rest of Moldova. Visitors to Tiraspol can explore its Soviet-era monuments, government buildings, and military memorials, as well as its bustling markets, parks, and squares.

Overall, a journey through Moldova's historic cities is a journey through time and space, where the past meets the present in a captivating tapestry of culture, heritage, and tradition. Whether exploring the bustling streets of Chisinau, the tranquil landscapes of Orhei, the industrial heartland of Balti, or the political intrigue of Tiraspol, visitors to Moldova's cities are sure to be enchanted by the sights, sounds, and stories that await them at every turn.

Chisinau: The Vibrant Capital City

Welcome to Chisinau, the vibrant capital city of Moldova, where the past meets the present in a bustling urban landscape brimming with culture, history, and charm. Situated in the heart of the country, Chisinau is a dynamic metropolis that serves as the political, economic, and cultural center of Moldova.

Founded in the 15th century, Chisinau has a rich and storied history that is reflected in its diverse architectural styles, from elegant neoclassical buildings to Soviet-era apartment blocks and modern skyscrapers. The city's skyline is dominated by landmarks such as the Nativity Cathedral, a stunning Orthodox church with a distinctive green dome that rises majestically above the cityscape.

Chisinau is also home to a wealth of cultural institutions, including theaters, museums, and galleries, that showcase the country's artistic heritage and creative talent. The National Museum of History of Moldova offers visitors a fascinating glimpse into the country's past, with exhibits that span thousands of years of human civilization, while the National Opera and Ballet Theater delights audiences with world-class performances of opera, ballet, and classical music.

But Chisinau is not just a city of history and culture—it is also a thriving hub of commerce, industry, and innovation. The city is home to numerous businesses, startups, and tech companies that are driving economic growth and development in Moldova, while its bustling markets, shopping malls, and restaurants offer residents and visitors alike a taste of the vibrant urban lifestyle.

Chisinau's parks and green spaces provide respite from the hustle and bustle of city life, with sprawling parks such as Stefan cel Mare Central Park and Valea Morilor Park offering opportunities for recreation, relaxation, and outdoor activities. The city's botanical garden, founded in 1950, is a haven for nature lovers, with thousands of plant species from around the world that thrive in its lush and verdant surroundings.

Overall, Chisinau is a city of contrasts and contradictions, where ancient traditions coexist with modern aspirations, and where the past and the present converge in a vibrant tapestry of culture, history, and life. Whether exploring its historic landmarks, sampling its culinary delights, or simply soaking in the atmosphere of its bustling streets, visitors to Chisinau are sure to be captivated by the city's unique charm and allure.

Tiraspol: Exploring Transnistria's Enigmatic Capital

Welcome to Tiraspol, the enigmatic capital of Transnistria, a region with a unique history and identity that sets it apart from the rest of Moldova. Situated on the eastern bank of the Dniester River, Tiraspol is a city steeped in political intrigue and cultural complexity, where the echoes of the Soviet past mingle with the rhythms of modern life.

Founded in the 18th century by Russian settlers, Tiraspol has a rich and storied history that is reflected in its architecture, monuments, and cultural traditions. The city's streets are lined with Soviet-era buildings, government offices, and military memorials, while its parks, squares, and boulevards offer residents and visitors alike a glimpse into the city's past and present.

One of the most iconic landmarks in Tiraspol is the Transnistrian Parliament building, a grand neoclassical structure that serves as the seat of government for the breakaway region. The parliament building, with its imposing columns and ornate façade, is a symbol of Transnistria's political aspirations and desire for independence from Moldova.

Another must-see attraction in Tiraspol is the Monument to Suvorov, a towering statue of the Russian military commander Alexander Suvorov that stands proudly in the city center. The monument, which was erected in 1979 to commemorate the 200th anniversary of Suvorov's victory over the Ottoman Empire, is a symbol of Tiraspol's ties to Russia and its military heritage.

In addition to its political and military landmarks, Tiraspol is also home to a vibrant cultural scene, with theaters, museums, and galleries that showcase the region's artistic heritage and creative talent. The Tiraspol Drama Theater, founded in 1940, is one of the oldest theaters in Transnistria, offering performances of plays, operas, and ballets that celebrate the country's cultural identity and traditions.

Tiraspol's markets, shops, and cafes are also worth exploring, offering visitors the chance to sample local delicacies, purchase traditional crafts, and immerse themselves in the everyday life of the city. The Central Market, located in the heart of Tiraspol, is a bustling hub of activity, with vendors selling fresh produce, meats, cheeses, and other goods from around the region.

Overall, Tiraspol is a city of contrasts and contradictions, where the legacy of the Soviet past coexists with the aspirations of the present, and where the enigmatic allure of Transnistria is on full display. Whether exploring its historic landmarks, experiencing its cultural treasures, or simply soaking in the atmosphere of its streets, visitors to Tiraspol are sure to be captivated by the city's unique charm and intrigue.

Balti: Moldova's Northern Hub of Commerce and Culture

Welcome to Balti, Moldova's dynamic northern hub of commerce and culture, where tradition meets innovation in a city that pulsates with energy and vitality. Situated in the northern part of the country, Balti is the second-largest city in Moldova and a major center of industry, commerce, and education.

Founded in the 15th century, Balti has a rich history that is reflected in its diverse architectural styles and cultural heritage. The city's skyline is dominated by a mix of Soviet-era apartment blocks, elegant 19th-century mansions, and modern high-rise buildings, creating a unique blend of old and new that is characteristic of Balti's urban landscape.

Balti is known for its thriving commercial sector, with bustling markets, shopping centers, and businesses that drive economic activity in the region. The city is home to numerous factories, warehouses, and industrial facilities that produce a wide range of goods, including textiles, machinery, and food products.

In addition to its industrial prowess, Balti is also a center of cultural and educational excellence, with schools, universities, and cultural institutions that serve the needs of residents and visitors alike. The

Balti State University, founded in 1945, is one of the largest and most prestigious universities in Moldova, offering a wide range of academic programs and research opportunities.

Balti's cultural scene is vibrant and diverse, with theaters, museums, and galleries that showcase the city's artistic heritage and creative talent. The Balti Dramatic Theater, founded in 1953, is one of the oldest theaters in the country, offering performances of plays, operas, and ballets that entertain and inspire audiences of all ages.

But Balti is not just a city of industry and culture—it is also a place of natural beauty and outdoor recreation. The city is surrounded by picturesque countryside, with rolling hills, lush forests, and meandering rivers that offer opportunities for hiking, camping, and other outdoor activities.

Overall, Balti is a city of contrasts and contradictions, where the hustle and bustle of urban life coexist with the tranquility of the countryside, and where the past and the present converge in a dynamic tapestry of commerce, culture, and community. Whether exploring its industrial landmarks, enjoying its cultural treasures, or simply soaking in the beauty of its natural surroundings, visitors to Balti are sure to be captivated by the city's unique charm and vitality.

Cahul: A Southern Gem by the Prut River

Welcome to Cahul, a charming southern gem nestled along the banks of the Prut River in Moldova. This picturesque city, with its rich history, stunning landscapes, and vibrant culture, is a hidden treasure waiting to be discovered by visitors from near and far.

Founded in the 15th century, Cahul has a long and storied past that is reflected in its architecture, monuments, and cultural traditions. The city's historic center is a maze of cobblestone streets, colorful buildings, and quaint cafes, where visitors can wander and explore at their leisure, soaking in the atmosphere of this charming corner of Moldova.

Cahul is known for its stunning natural beauty, with the Prut River winding its way through the city and surrounding countryside, offering opportunities for boating, fishing, and other water-based activities. The nearby Cahul Lake, formed by the damming of the Prut River, is a popular destination for outdoor enthusiasts, with its pristine waters and scenic vistas attracting visitors year-round.

In addition to its natural attractions, Cahul is also home to a variety of cultural and historical landmarks that showcase the city's rich heritage.

The Cahul History Museum, housed in a beautiful 19th-century mansion, offers visitors a fascinating glimpse into the city's past, with exhibits that explore its ancient origins, medieval history, and modern development.

One of the most iconic landmarks in Cahul is the St. Nicholas Church, a stunning Orthodox cathedral that dates back to the 19th century and serves as a symbol of the city's religious heritage and spiritual significance. The cathedral's intricate architecture, colorful frescoes, and ornate iconography make it a must-see destination for visitors to Cahul.

Cahul is also a center of cultural and artistic activity, with theaters, galleries, and performance spaces that showcase the talents of local artists and performers. The Cahul Drama Theater, founded in 1953, offers a diverse program of plays, concerts, and dance performances that entertain and inspire audiences of all ages.

Overall, Cahul is a city of charm and beauty, where history and nature converge in a harmonious blend of past and present. Whether exploring its historic landmarks, enjoying its natural attractions, or simply soaking in the atmosphere of its bustling streets, visitors to Cahul are sure to be captivated by the city's unique charm and allure.

Bender: A Tale of Fortresses and Crossroads

Welcome to Bender, a city steeped in history and intrigue, where fortresses stand as silent sentinels of the past and crossroads converge to tell tales of ancient civilizations and modern conflicts. Situated on the banks of the Dniester River in the breakaway region of Transnistria, Bender has been a strategic stronghold for centuries, with its strategic location at the crossroads of Eastern Europe making it a coveted prize for empires and armies throughout history.

The city's most iconic landmark is the Bender Fortress, a sprawling complex of walls, towers, and bastions that dates back to the 16th century. Built by the Ottoman Empire to defend its southern borders, the fortress has witnessed countless battles and sieges over the centuries, serving as a key military outpost and trading hub for the region.

Bender's history is intertwined with that of the surrounding region, which has been inhabited since ancient times by a diverse array of cultures and civilizations. Archaeological excavations in and around Bender have revealed traces of ancient Greek, Roman, and Byzantine settlements, as well as artifacts from the medieval period and beyond.

In the 19th century, Bender became part of the Russian Empire and was transformed into a bustling commercial center, with merchants and traders flocking to the city to buy and sell goods from across Europe and Asia. The city's strategic importance was further solidified during the Russo-Turkish Wars, when it served as a vital supply base and military stronghold for the Russian army.

During the Soviet era, Bender was a thriving industrial city, with factories, warehouses, and manufacturing plants that produced a wide range of goods, including textiles, machinery, and food products. The city's population swelled as workers from across the Soviet Union came to seek employment and opportunity in the bustling metropolis.

Today, Bender is a city of contrasts, where the legacy of the past coexists with the realities of the present. The Bender Fortress still stands as a testament to the city's storied history, while modern developments and infrastructure projects are transforming the urban landscape and shaping the future of the city.

But despite its tumultuous past and uncertain present, Bender remains a place of resilience and resilience, where the spirit of its people shines through in the face of adversity. Whether exploring its historic landmarks, learning about its rich cultural heritage, or simply soaking in the atmosphere of its bustling streets, visitors to Bender are sure to be captivated by the city's unique blend of fortresses and crossroads.

Soroca: The Gypsy Capital of Moldova

Welcome to Soroca, a city in northern Moldova known as the "Gypsy Capital" for its significant Romani population and cultural influence. Situated on the banks of the Dniester River, Soroca is a melting pot of cultures, where traditions from across Eastern Europe and beyond come together to create a vibrant and eclectic community.

The Romani people, also known as Gypsies, have a long and storied history in Soroca, dating back centuries to their migration from India to Europe. Today, Soroca is home to one of the largest Romani communities in Moldova, with an estimated population of over 10,000 people.

The Romani population of Soroca is known for its rich cultural heritage, including traditional music, dance, and craftsmanship. Visitors to the city can experience firsthand the vibrant sights and sounds of Romani culture at the local markets, where colorful clothing, handmade jewelry, and other crafts are on display.

One of the most iconic landmarks in Soroca is the Soroca Fortress, a medieval stronghold that dates back to the 15th century. Built by the Moldavian prince Stephen the Great, the fortress served as a key defensive outpost and trading center for the region, with its strategic location on the banks of the Dniester River making it an important stronghold for centuries.

In addition to its Romani population and historic fortress, Soroca is also known for its picturesque landscapes, with rolling hills, vineyards, and orchards that stretch as far as the eye can see. The surrounding countryside is a haven for outdoor enthusiasts, with opportunities for hiking, biking, and birdwatching in the nearby Codrii Forest and Dniester River Valley.

Soroca is also a center of commerce and industry, with factories, warehouses, and agricultural facilities that contribute to the region's economy. The city's proximity to the Ukrainian border makes it an important hub for trade and transportation, with goods flowing in and out of the country via road, rail, and river.

Overall, Soroca is a city of contrasts and contradictions, where the ancient traditions of the Romani people blend seamlessly with the modern realities of life in Moldova. Whether exploring its historic landmarks, experiencing its vibrant culture, or simply soaking in the beauty of its natural surroundings, visitors to Soroca are sure to be captivated by the city's unique charm and allure.

Orhei: A Journey to the Ancient Past

Welcome to Orhei, a city in central Moldova that takes you on a captivating journey to the ancient past. Situated on the banks of the Raut River, Orhei is a place where history comes alive, with traces of human civilization dating back thousands of years.

Orhei is renowned for its stunning natural beauty, with rolling hills, lush vineyards, and dramatic limestone cliffs that overlook the river valley. The surrounding countryside is dotted with ancient cave complexes, archaeological sites, and religious landmarks that bear witness to the city's rich and varied history.

One of the most iconic landmarks in Orhei is the Orheiul Vechi Monastery Complex, a sprawling complex of caves, churches, and fortifications that date back to the 13th century. Carved into the limestone cliffs overlooking the Raut River, the monastery complex is a testament to the religious and cultural heritage of the region, with its ancient frescoes, intricate carvings, and stunning views of the surrounding countryside.

In addition to its religious significance, Orhei is also home to numerous archaeological sites that offer insights into the city's ancient past. Excavations in and around Orhei have uncovered traces of ancient settlements dating back to the Neolithic period, as well as artifacts from the Bronze Age, Iron Age, and medieval period.

One of the most notable archaeological sites in Orhei is the Butuceni Archaeological Complex, a sprawling complex of ancient dwellings, tombs, and fortifications that date back to the 4th century BC. The complex offers visitors the opportunity to explore the ruins of ancient houses, temples, and defensive structures, as well as learn about the daily lives of the people who inhabited the area thousands of years ago.

Orhei is also a center of cultural and artistic activity, with theaters, museums, and galleries that showcase the region's artistic heritage and creative talent. The Orhei Museum of History and Ethnography, founded in 1959, offers visitors a fascinating glimpse into the city's past, with exhibits that explore its ancient origins, medieval history, and modern development.

Overall, Orhei is a city of contrasts and contradictions, where the ancient traditions of the past blend seamlessly with the modern realities of life in Moldova. Whether exploring its historic landmarks, experiencing its vibrant culture, or simply soaking in the beauty of its natural surroundings, visitors to Orhei are sure to be captivated by the city's unique charm and allure.

Gagauzia: Unveiling Moldova's Cultural Diversity

Welcome to Gagauzia, a region in southern Moldova that unveils the rich tapestry of cultural diversity within the country. Situated between the Dniester River and the Ukrainian border, Gagauzia is a unique blend of traditions, languages, and customs that reflects its complex history and diverse population.

The Gagauz people, an ethnic group of Turkic origin, are the predominant population in Gagauzia, with their own distinct language, culture, and identity. Gagauzia is recognized as an autonomous territorial unit within Moldova, with its own elected assembly and cultural institutions that promote and preserve the Gagauz heritage.

The capital city of Gagauzia is Comrat, a bustling urban center that serves as the administrative, economic, and cultural hub of the region. Founded in the 19th century by Russian settlers, Comrat is home to numerous government buildings, businesses, and cultural institutions that showcase the unique identity of Gagauzia. One of the most iconic landmarks in Comrat is the Gagauz National Assembly building, a grand neoclassical structure that houses the region's legislative body. The assembly is responsible for governing Gagauzia and promoting its cultural, linguistic, and historical heritage.

Gagauzia is also known for its vibrant cultural scene, with festivals, celebrations, and events that showcase the traditions and customs of the Gagauz people. The Gagauz National Day, celebrated on October 19th, is a major holiday in the region, with parades, concerts, and traditional performances that highlight the rich cultural heritage of Gagauzia. In addition to its Gagauz population, Gagauzia is also home to other ethnic groups, including Ukrainians, Russians, Bulgarians, and Moldovans, who contribute to the region's cultural diversity and heritage. The languages spoken in Gagauzia include Gagauz, Russian, Ukrainian, and Moldovan, reflecting the multicultural and multilingual nature of the region.

Gagauzia is also known for its picturesque landscapes, with rolling hills, fertile plains, and vineyards that produce some of the finest wines in Moldova. The region's agricultural sector is a key contributor to its economy, with crops such as wheat, corn, sunflowers, and grapes grown on the fertile land.

Overall, Gagauzia is a region of cultural richness and diversity, where the traditions of the past meet the realities of the present in a vibrant and dynamic tapestry of heritage and identity. Whether exploring its historic landmarks, experiencing its cultural traditions, or simply enjoying its natural beauty, visitors to Gagauzia are sure to be captivated by the region's unique charm and allure.

Moldova's Spiritual Heritage: Churches, Monasteries, and Synagogues

Welcome to Moldova's spiritual heritage, a landscape adorned with churches, monasteries, and synagogues that reflect the diverse religious traditions and cultural history of the country. Moldova, nestled in the heart of Eastern Europe, is a land where faith has played a significant role in shaping its identity and communities for centuries.

Orthodox Christianity is the predominant religion in Moldova, with the majority of the population adhering to the Eastern Orthodox faith. The country is home to numerous Orthodox churches and monasteries, many of which date back hundreds of years and are revered as sacred sites by believers. The Capriana Monastery, founded in the 15th century, is one such example, renowned for its beautiful architecture and spiritual significance.

In addition to Orthodox Christianity, Moldova is also home to other religious communities, including Catholics, Protestants, Jews, and Muslims. Each of these communities has left its mark on the country's spiritual landscape, with churches, synagogues, mosques, and other places of worship scattered throughout the land.

Catholicism has a long history in Moldova, with roots dating back to the medieval period. The country is home to several Catholic churches and cathedrals, including the Assumption Cathedral in Chisinau, which serves as the main cathedral of the Roman Catholic Church in Moldova.

Judaism has also played a significant role in Moldova's spiritual heritage, with Jewish communities thriving in various parts of the country for centuries. The Jewish Cemetery in Chisinau, with its elaborate tombstones and memorials, is a poignant reminder of the rich Jewish history and heritage in Moldova.

Moldova is also home to a small but vibrant Muslim community, with mosques and Islamic cultural centers found in cities and towns across the country. The Haji Ali Mosque in Chisinau, built in the early 19th century, is one of the oldest mosques in Moldova and serves as a focal point for the Muslim community.

Overall, Moldova's spiritual heritage is a testament to the country's rich and diverse cultural tapestry, where faith has served as a source of inspiration, comfort, and unity for generations. Whether exploring its historic churches, monasteries, and synagogues, or witnessing the vibrant religious life of its communities, visitors to Moldova are sure to be moved by the depth and diversity of its spiritual heritage.

Moldova's Wine Legacy: Nectar of the Gods

Welcome to Moldova's wine legacy, a story as old as time itself and a tradition deeply ingrained in the culture and identity of the nation. Nestled between Romania and Ukraine in Eastern Europe, Moldova boasts a rich and storied history of winemaking that spans millennia.

The roots of Moldova's winemaking tradition can be traced back to ancient times, with evidence of grape cultivation and wine production dating back over 5,000 years. The favorable climate, fertile soil, and gentle slopes of the Moldovan countryside provide the perfect conditions for growing grapes and producing high-quality wines.

Moldova is home to over 250,000 acres of vineyards, making it one of the largest wine-producing countries in the world per capita. The country's diverse terroir, which includes both continental and maritime climates, allows for the cultivation of a wide variety of grape varietals, from indigenous varieties such as Feteasca Neagra and Rara Neagra to international favorites like Chardonnay and Cabernet Sauvignon.

The wine industry plays a significant role in Moldova's economy, with wine production and exportation contributing to both GDP and employment. The country is renowned for its high-quality wines, which have won numerous awards and accolades on the international stage.

One of Moldova's most famous wine regions is the Codru region, located in the center of the country. Known for its picturesque landscapes and historic vineyards, Codru is home to some of Moldova's oldest wineries and most renowned wine producers.

Another notable wine region in Moldova is the Purcari region, located in the south-eastern part of the country near the border with Ukraine. Purcari is famous for its red wines, particularly its Cabernet Sauvignon and Merlot blends, which have gained recognition and acclaim around the world.

In addition to its commercial wineries, Moldova is also home to numerous underground wine cellars, known as "milestii mici" or "Cricova," where thousands of barrels of wine are aged in underground tunnels that stretch for miles beneath the earth's surface. These cellars are not only a testament to Moldova's winemaking heritage but also a popular tourist attraction, drawing visitors from around the world to sample the country's finest wines in a unique and unforgettable setting.

Overall, Moldova's wine legacy is a source of pride and passion for the people of the nation, a symbol of resilience, tradition, and craftsmanship that continues to thrive and evolve with each passing generation. Whether exploring its historic vineyards, sampling its award-winning wines, or simply soaking in the beauty of its wine country landscapes, visitors to Moldova are sure to be captivated by the magic of its wine legacy.

Moldovan Wineries: Exploring the Wine Routes

Welcome to Moldovan wineries, where every bottle tells a story and every sip is a journey through the rich tapestry of Moldova's winemaking heritage. Nestled between rolling hills and picturesque vineyards, Moldova's wineries offer visitors the opportunity to explore the country's diverse terroir and experience the passion and craftsmanship that goes into each bottle of wine.

One of the most popular wine routes in Moldova is the "Wine Road of Moldova," a scenic route that winds its way through the country's most renowned wine regions, including Codru, Purcari, and Milestii Mici. Along the way, visitors can stop at wineries, vineyards, and wine cellars to sample a wide variety of wines, from crisp whites and fruity rosés to full-bodied reds and sparkling cuvées.

Each winery along the wine route offers its own unique blend of history, tradition, and innovation, with guided tours and tastings that provide insight into the winemaking process and the culture of wine in Moldova. Visitors can learn about the different grape varietals grown in the region, explore the vineyards where the grapes are grown, and witness firsthand the age-old techniques and modern technologies used to produce some of the finest wines in the world.

One of the highlights of any wine tour in Moldova is a visit to the underground wine cellars, known as "milestii mici" or "Cricova," where thousands of barrels of wine are aged in underground tunnels that stretch for miles beneath the earth's surface. These cellars are not only a testament to Moldova's winemaking heritage but also a unique and unforgettable setting for wine tastings and events.

In addition to the Wine Road of Moldova, there are numerous other wine routes and trails throughout the country that offer visitors the chance to explore Moldova's diverse wine regions and discover hidden gems off the beaten path. Whether exploring the historic vineyards of Cricova, the scenic landscapes of Purcari, or the charming wineries of Codru, there's something for every wine lover to discover and enjoy in Moldova's wine country.

Overall, Moldova's wineries offer visitors a truly immersive and unforgettable experience, where the beauty of the countryside, the warmth of the people, and the magic of winemaking come together to create memories that will last a lifetime. So grab a glass, raise a toast, and let the journey begin!

Moldova's Soviet Legacy: Traces of a Bygone Era

Welcome to Moldova's Soviet legacy, a chapter of history that has left an indelible mark on the country's landscape, culture, and identity. Situated between Romania and Ukraine in Eastern Europe, Moldova spent much of the 20th century under Soviet rule, a period that profoundly shaped its development and character.

The Soviet Union annexed Moldova, then known as Bessarabia, in 1940, following the Molotov-Ribbentrop Pact between Nazi Germany and the Soviet Union. This marked the beginning of a tumultuous period of Sovietization for Moldova, during which the country underwent significant political, social, and economic transformation.

Under Soviet rule, Moldova experienced rapid industrialization and urbanization, with factories, collective farms, and industrial complexes springing up across the countryside. The capital city of Chisinau, in particular, saw a dramatic expansion of its infrastructure, with new buildings, roads, and public amenities built to accommodate the growing population.

The Soviet government also implemented a policy of Russification in Moldova, promoting the Russian language and culture at the expense of the country's indigenous languages and traditions. Russian became the dominant language of government, education, and media, while Moldovan, a dialect of Romanian, was relegated to secondary status.

Despite the efforts of the Soviet authorities to suppress Moldova's national identity, elements of the country's cultural heritage and traditions persisted. Folk music, dance, and literature remained important expressions of Moldovan identity, while religious observance continued to play a central role in the lives of many Moldovans, despite official atheistic policies.

The Soviet era also left its mark on Moldova's built environment, with numerous examples of Soviet architecture and urban planning still visible in cities and towns across the country. Brutalist apartment blocks, government buildings, and monuments to Soviet leaders dot the landscape, serving as tangible reminders of Moldova's communist past.

One of the most enduring legacies of the Soviet era in Moldova is the Transnistrian conflict, a separatist movement that erupted in the early 1990s following the collapse of the Soviet

Union. Transnistria, a breakaway region in eastern Moldova, declared independence in 1990, sparking a brief but bloody conflict with Moldovan forces.

Today, Moldova is a country in transition, grappling with the legacy of its Soviet past while striving to build a brighter future. The scars of the past are still visible, but Moldova's people are resilient, and their spirit and determination are driving the country forward towards a new era of prosperity and progress.

Moldova's Independence Square: Symbol of National Sovereignty

Welcome to Independence Square, the beating heart of Moldova's capital city, Chisinau, and a symbol of the nation's hard-fought journey to sovereignty and self-determination. Situated in the heart of the city, Independence Square, also known as Piața Marii Adunări Naționale, serves as a gathering place for citizens, a center of political activity, and a focal point for national celebrations and events.

Originally laid out in the early 19th century, Independence Square has undergone numerous transformations over the years, reflecting the changing political, social, and cultural landscape of Moldova. In the center of the square stands the iconic Triumphal Arch, a symbol of Moldova's struggle for independence and resilience in the face of adversity.

Surrounding the square are numerous historic buildings, including the Government House, the National History Museum of Moldova, and the Cathedral of Christ's Nativity, which add to the square's architectural grandeur and cultural significance. The square is also home to numerous statues, monuments, and memorials that pay tribute to Moldova's rich history and heritage.

Independence Square has played a central role in many key moments in Moldova's history, including the declaration of independence from the Soviet Union on August 27, 1991. Tens of thousands of Moldovans gathered in the square to celebrate this historic occasion, waving flags, singing patriotic songs, and expressing their hopes and aspirations for the future.

In addition to its historical significance, Independence Square is also a vibrant and bustling hub of activity, with cafes, restaurants, shops, and markets lining its streets. Visitors to the square can sample traditional Moldovan cuisine, shop for souvenirs and handicrafts, or simply soak in the atmosphere and watch the world go by.

Throughout the year, Independence Square plays host to a variety of events and festivals, including concerts, parades, and cultural performances that showcase the rich diversity of Moldovan culture and traditions. From Independence Day celebrations to Victory Day commemorations, the square is a place where Moldovans come together to celebrate their shared heritage and identity.

Overall, Independence Square is more than just a physical space – it is a symbol of Moldova's resilience, determination, and commitment to freedom and democracy. As the country continues to navigate its path forward, Independence Square will remain a cherished landmark and a testament to the strength and spirit of the Moldovan people.

Exploring Moldova's Archaeological Sites: Unearthing Ancient Treasures

Welcome to the world of Moldovan archaeology, where every shovel of dirt has the potential to uncover ancient treasures and shed light on the country's rich and diverse history. Moldova, situated at the crossroads of Eastern Europe, has been inhabited for thousands of years, and its soil is teeming with archaeological sites that offer a glimpse into the lives of its ancient inhabitants.

One of the most famous archaeological sites in Moldova is the Old Orhei Archaeological Complex, located on the banks of the Raut River near the village of Trebujeni. This site is home to the remains of a Neolithic settlement dating back over 6,000 years, as well as remnants of ancient fortifications, burial mounds, and religious structures. Another notable archaeological site in Moldova is the Cucuteni-Trypillian culture complex, which dates back to the Neolithic and Copper Age periods. This culture, characterized by its distinctive pottery and elaborate settlements, flourished in the region between 5500 and 2750 BCE, leaving behind a rich archaeological legacy that continues to be studied and explored by researchers today. Moldova is also home to numerous ancient fortresses and citadels, which served as important centers of trade, defense, and governance throughout the country's history. One such fortress is the Soroca Fortress, located in the northern part of the country, which dates back to the late 15th century and is one of the best-preserved medieval fortresses in Eastern Europe. In addition to its ancient settlements and fortifications, Moldova is also rich in archaeological artifacts, including pottery, jewelry, tools, and weapons, which offer insights into the daily lives and material culture of its ancient inhabitants. These artifacts are housed in museums and archaeological repositories throughout the country, where they are studied and preserved for future generations.

One of the challenges facing Moldovan archaeology is the preservation and protection of its archaeological sites and artifacts. Illegal excavation, looting, and development pose significant threats to the country's cultural heritage, and efforts are underway to raise awareness and implement measures to safeguard these valuable resources.

Despite these challenges, Moldova's archaeological sites continue to be a source of fascination and discovery for researchers, historians, and enthusiasts alike. With ongoing excavations, research projects, and conservation efforts, the country's ancient treasures are sure to reveal even more secrets and surprises in the years to come.

The Moldovan Language: A Linguistic Journey

Welcome to the linguistic journey of the Moldovan language, a fascinating and complex tapestry woven from centuries of history, culture, and tradition. Moldovan, also known as Moldovan Romanian, is the official language of Moldova and shares many similarities with the Romanian language spoken in neighboring Romania.

Linguistically, Moldovan is a Romance language, belonging to the same family as French, Italian, Spanish, and Portuguese. It is derived from Latin, the language of the ancient Romans, and has evolved over time through various influences from neighboring languages and cultures.

The Moldovan language is written using the Latin alphabet, with a few additional letters and diacritical marks to represent sounds that are unique to the language. The alphabet consists of 31 letters, including the standard Latin letters A-Z as well as additional letters such as ă, â, î, and ș.

One of the defining features of the Moldovan language is its close relationship with Romanian. While some linguists consider Moldovan and Romanian to be separate languages, others view them as dialects of the same language. Both languages share a common vocabulary, grammar, and syntax, with minor differences in pronunciation and spelling. Moldovan has been heavily influenced by other languages and cultures throughout its history, including Slavic languages such as Russian and Ukrainian, as well as Turkish, Greek, and Hungarian. These influences can be seen in the vocabulary, phonology, and syntax of the language, which has borrowed words and expressions from various linguistic sources.

Despite these influences, Moldovan remains distinct in its own right, with a rich literary tradition, a vibrant oral culture, and a growing body of academic research and scholarship. The language is spoken by the majority of the population in Moldova and is used in government, education, media, and everyday communication.

In recent years, there has been a renewed interest in promoting the Moldovan language and fostering a sense of linguistic identity and pride among its speakers. Efforts have been made to standardize the language, develop educational materials, and promote its use in all aspects of public life.

Overall, the Moldovan language is a testament to the rich cultural heritage and linguistic diversity of Moldova, reflecting the country's history, identity, and aspirations for the future. As Moldova continues to evolve and grow, so too will its language, serving as a bridge between the past and the present, and a beacon of unity and belonging for its people.

Moldovan Literature: Exploring National Voices

Welcome to the world of Moldovan literature, a rich and diverse tapestry of voices that reflects the country's history, culture, and identity. Moldovan literature has a long and storied tradition, dating back centuries to the oral poetry and folk tales of its indigenous people.

One of the earliest forms of Moldovan literature is epic poetry, which was passed down orally from generation to generation and celebrated the heroic deeds and legendary figures of Moldovan history. These epic poems, known as "duma" or "balada," were often performed by traveling bards and storytellers and served as a means of preserving and transmitting the cultural heritage of the Moldovan people.

In the 19th and early 20th centuries, Moldovan literature began to emerge as a distinct literary tradition, with writers and poets such as Alexei Mateevici, Mihai Eminescu, and Alecu Russo leading the way. These literary figures drew inspiration from Moldova's landscape, history, and folklore, crafting works that celebrated the beauty of the countryside, the resilience of the people, and the quest for national identity and independence.

One of the most famous works of Moldovan literature is "Miorița," a ballad written by the poet Vasile Alecsandri in the mid-19th century. The poem tells the story of a young shepherd who is betrayed by his fellow shepherds and left to die, but who finds solace in the song of a magical sheep. "Miorița" is considered a masterpiece of Romanian literature and has been translated into numerous languages.

In the Soviet era, Moldovan literature experienced a period of censorship and repression, as the communist regime sought to control the cultural narrative and promote socialist realism as the dominant literary style. Despite these challenges, writers such as Grigore Vieru and Emilian Galaicu-Păun continued to produce works that explored themes of national identity, social justice, and human dignity.

Since gaining independence in 1991, Moldovan literature has experienced a renaissance, with writers and poets exploring new themes, styles, and forms of expression. Contemporary authors such as Ion Druță, Dumitru Crudu, and Ana Blandiana continue to push the boundaries of Moldovan literature, addressing pressing social issues, challenging established norms, and engaging with the complexities of modern life.

Overall, Moldovan literature is a vibrant and dynamic field that continues to evolve and thrive, reflecting the ever-changing landscape of Moldovan society and culture. From its ancient roots in oral tradition to its modern manifestations in novels, poetry, and drama, Moldovan literature offers a window into the soul of the nation and a testament to the enduring power of the written word.

Moldova's Educational System: Nurturing Future Generations

Welcome to the educational landscape of Moldova, where the seeds of knowledge are sown and the future generations are nurtured to reach their fullest potential. Moldova's educational system is a cornerstone of the nation's development, providing students with the tools they need to succeed in an ever-changing world.

The Moldovan educational system is structured into three main levels: preschool education, primary and secondary education, and higher education. Preschool education is optional and typically begins at the age of three, providing young children with a foundation in social skills, basic literacy, and numeracy.

Primary and secondary education in Moldova is compulsory and spans nine years, divided into four years of primary education and five years of lower secondary education. The curriculum includes a range of subjects, including mathematics, science, language arts, social studies, and physical education, with an emphasis on developing critical thinking, problem-solving, and communication skills.

At the end of lower secondary education, students take a national examination known as the Baccalaureate, which assesses their knowledge and skills in core subjects. Successful completion of the Baccalaureate exam is required for entry into higher education institutions in Moldova.

Higher education in Moldova is offered at universities, academies, and institutes across the country, with a wide range of undergraduate and graduate programs available in various fields of study. The most prestigious universities in Moldova include the Moldova State University, the Technical University of Moldova, and the Academy of Sciences of Moldova.

In recent years, Moldova has made significant strides in expanding access to higher education and improving the quality of its educational institutions. Efforts have been made to modernize the curriculum, enhance teaching methods, and increase opportunities for student mobility and international collaboration.

Despite these efforts, Moldova's educational system still faces numerous challenges, including limited resources, outdated infrastructure, and disparities in access to quality education between urban and rural areas. Additionally, corruption and political interference in the education sector remain persistent issues that threaten to undermine the integrity and effectiveness of the system.

Nevertheless, Moldova's educational system continues to play a vital role in shaping the country's future, empowering individuals to achieve their dreams and contribute to the social, cultural, and economic development of the nation. With ongoing reforms and investments in education, Moldova is striving to create a brighter future for its citizens and future generations to come.

Moldova's Healthcare System: Ensuring Well-being for All

Welcome to the realm of Moldova's healthcare system, a crucial pillar in safeguarding the well-being and vitality of its citizens. Moldova's healthcare system is a blend of public and private sectors, striving to provide accessible and high-quality medical services to all residents, regardless of their socioeconomic status.

The healthcare system in Moldova is primarily funded through a combination of government allocations, social health insurance contributions, and out-of-pocket payments by patients. The Ministry of Health is responsible for overseeing and regulating the healthcare sector, setting policies, and allocating resources to ensure the delivery of essential health services across the country.

Primary healthcare in Moldova is provided through a network of community-based health centers, polyclinics, and family medicine practices, which serve as the first point of contact for patients seeking medical care. These facilities offer a wide range of services, including preventive care, routine check-ups, vaccinations, and treatment for common illnesses and chronic conditions.

In addition to primary care, Moldova boasts a network of specialized hospitals, clinics, and medical centers that provide secondary and tertiary care services, including surgery, specialized diagnostics, and treatment for complex medical conditions. These facilities are equipped with modern medical equipment and staffed by skilled healthcare professionals trained in various medical specialties.

Moldova's healthcare system also places a strong emphasis on preventive medicine and public health initiatives aimed at promoting healthy behaviors, preventing disease, and reducing the burden of illness in the population. These initiatives include health education campaigns, vaccination programs, screening for chronic diseases, and efforts to address social determinants of health such as poverty, unemployment, and access to clean water and sanitation.

Despite these efforts, Moldova's healthcare system faces numerous challenges, including inadequate funding, a shortage of medical personnel, outdated infrastructure, and disparities in access to care between urban and rural areas. Additionally, the country's healthcare system has been strained by the COVID-19 pandemic, highlighting the need for investment in healthcare infrastructure, workforce development, and pandemic preparedness.

Nevertheless, Moldova's healthcare system remains committed to its mission of ensuring the well-being and health of all its citizens. With ongoing reforms, investments, and international collaboration, Moldova is striving to build a stronger, more resilient healthcare system that meets the evolving needs of its population and fosters a healthier future for all.

Moldova's Economy: From Agriculture to Technology

Welcome to the dynamic landscape of Moldova's economy, a story of resilience, transformation, and diversification. Moldova, a small landlocked country in Eastern Europe, has undergone significant changes in its economic structure over the years, evolving from a predominantly agricultural economy to one that is increasingly driven by technology and innovation.

Agriculture has long been the backbone of Moldova's economy, with fertile soil and favorable climatic conditions supporting the cultivation of a wide range of crops, including grapes, fruits, vegetables, grains, and sunflower seeds. The agricultural sector remains an important contributor to the country's GDP, employing a significant portion of the population and generating export revenue through the sale of agricultural products to international markets.

In addition to agriculture, Moldova's economy has diversified into other sectors, including manufacturing, services, and information technology. The manufacturing sector encompasses a variety of industries, including food processing, textiles, machinery, and electronics, with companies producing goods for both domestic consumption and export to foreign markets.

The services sector in Moldova has also experienced growth in recent years, driven by the expansion of banking, finance, telecommunications, and tourism. Moldova's banking sector, in particular, has undergone significant reforms and modernization efforts, attracting foreign investment and contributing to the country's economic development.

Furthermore, Moldova is emerging as a regional hub for information technology and outsourcing services, with a growing number of software development companies, IT startups, and outsourcing firms establishing operations in the country. The government has implemented policies to promote the development of the IT sector, including tax incentives, investment incentives, and support for research and development activities.

Despite these advancements, Moldova's economy still faces numerous challenges, including corruption, political instability, inadequate infrastructure, and an underdeveloped business environment. Additionally, the country's economy has been impacted by external factors such as global economic downturns, regional conflicts, and the

COVID-19 pandemic, which have affected trade, investment, and economic growth.

Nevertheless, Moldova remains committed to fostering economic growth, innovation, and entrepreneurship, with the government implementing reforms to improve the business climate, attract foreign investment, and create opportunities for small and medium-sized enterprises. With its strategic location, skilled workforce, and commitment to reform, Moldova is well-positioned to continue its economic transformation and emerge as a competitive player in the global marketplace.

Moldova's Political Landscape: A Democratic Journey

Welcome to the complex terrain of Moldova's political landscape, a journey marked by transitions, challenges, and aspirations for democratic governance. Moldova, nestled between Romania and Ukraine, has navigated through various political systems and ideologies since gaining independence from the Soviet Union in 1991.

In its early years of independence, Moldova struggled to establish stable political institutions and forge a cohesive national identity. The country grappled with ethnic tensions, economic hardships, and political upheaval, as competing factions vied for power and influence.

The political landscape in Moldova is characterized by a multiparty system, with several political parties representing diverse interests and ideologies. The two main political blocs in Moldova are the pro-European Union (EU) parties, which advocate for closer ties with the West and reforms aimed at European integration, and the pro-Russian parties, which favor closer ties with Russia and prioritize maintaining traditional alliances.

The pro-European Union parties include the Party of Action and Solidarity (PAS), the Democratic Party of Moldova (PDM), and the Liberal Democratic Party (PLDM), among others. These parties have traditionally been associated with pro-Western policies, democratic reforms, and efforts to combat corruption and strengthen the rule of law.

On the other hand, the pro-Russian parties, such as the Party of Socialists of the Republic of Moldova (PSRM) and the Shor Party, advocate for closer economic and political ties with Russia and Eurasian integration initiatives. These parties often emphasize traditional values, national sovereignty, and economic cooperation with Russia and other post-Soviet states.

Moldova's political landscape is also influenced by geopolitical factors, with competing interests from Russia, the European Union, and the United States shaping the country's foreign policy and domestic politics. The issue of Transnistria, a breakaway region in eastern Moldova with a Russian-backed separatist government, adds a layer of complexity to Moldova's political dynamics and security challenges.

In recent years, Moldova has witnessed significant political developments, including mass protests, government collapses, and electoral controversies. The country has experienced periods of political instability and uncertainty, as well as moments of hope and progress toward democratic consolidation and reform.

Despite these challenges, Moldova remains committed to its democratic aspirations, with ongoing efforts to strengthen democratic institutions, promote transparency and accountability, and ensure free and fair elections. The country's democratic journey is a work in progress, shaped by the collective efforts of its citizens, political leaders, civil society organizations, and international partners. As Moldova continues on its path toward democratic governance, the resilience and determination of its people will undoubtedly shape the future of its political landscape.

Moldova's European Integration: Navigating Toward the Future

Welcome to the chapter on Moldova's European integration journey, a narrative of aspirations, challenges, and opportunities as the country seeks closer ties with the European Union (EU). Moldova, situated at the crossroads of Europe, has embarked on a path of European integration since gaining independence from the Soviet Union in 1991.

European integration has been a key foreign policy objective for Moldova, reflecting its desire to align with European values, norms, and standards, and to foster economic development, political stability, and regional cooperation. The European Union has been a key partner in Moldova's integration efforts, providing financial assistance, technical support, and diplomatic engagement to facilitate the country's progress toward European integration.

In 2014, Moldova signed an Association Agreement with the European Union, which includes provisions for political association and economic integration. The Association Agreement aims to deepen cooperation between Moldova and the EU in various areas, including trade, investment, governance, justice, and human rights. As part of the agreement,

Moldova has committed to implementing reforms aimed at strengthening democracy, rule of law, and market economy principles.

One of the key components of Moldova's European integration agenda is the Deep and Comprehensive Free Trade Area (DCFTA) with the European Union, which aims to liberalize trade between Moldova and the EU, harmonize regulations and standards, and promote economic modernization and competitiveness. The DCFTA provides Moldovan exporters with preferential access to the EU market, facilitating trade and investment flows and supporting economic growth and job creation.

Moldova's European integration efforts have faced challenges and setbacks, including political instability, corruption, and external pressures from Russia. The country has also grappled with internal divisions over its European orientation, with some political forces advocating for closer ties with Russia and Eurasian integration initiatives.

Nevertheless, Moldova has made significant progress in implementing reforms and aligning with European standards and practices. The country has adopted legislation and undertaken institutional changes to strengthen democratic institutions, improve governance and transparency, combat corruption, and protect human rights.

Moldova's European integration journey is ongoing, with the country continuing to pursue closer ties with the European Union and deepen its engagement with European institutions and member states. Despite the challenges and uncertainties, Moldova remains committed to its European aspirations, viewing European integration as a pathway to prosperity, stability, and a brighter future for its citizens.

Moldova's International Relations: Bridging East and West

Welcome to the intricate world of Moldova's international relations, where the country's geopolitical location and historical context shape its diplomatic engagements and foreign policy decisions. Moldova, nestled between Romania and Ukraine in Eastern Europe, serves as a bridge between the East and the West, navigating a complex web of regional dynamics and global interests.

At the heart of Moldova's international relations is its relationship with Russia, its former Soviet ally, and its aspirations for closer ties with the European Union and the United States. Moldova's history of Russian influence, combined with its desire for European integration, creates a delicate balancing act in its foreign policy approach.

On the one hand, Moldova maintains strong cultural, economic, and historical ties with Russia, which remains an important trading partner and political actor in the region. Moldova is a member of the Commonwealth of Independent States (CIS) and participates in various Russian-led integration initiatives, such as the Eurasian Economic Union and the Collective Security Treaty Organization.

On the other hand, Moldova has pursued closer ties with the European Union and the West, seeking to align with European values, norms, and standards, and to foster economic development, political stability, and democratic governance. Moldova signed an Association Agreement with the EU in 2014, which includes provisions for political association, economic integration, and visa liberalization.

Moldova's international relations are also influenced by its efforts to resolve the protracted conflict in Transnistria, a breakaway region in eastern Moldova with a Russian-backed separatist government. Moldova seeks to find a peaceful resolution to the Transnistrian conflict through diplomatic negotiations and international mediation efforts, involving the Organization for Security and Cooperation in Europe (OSCE), Russia, Ukraine, and the European Union.

In addition to its relations with Russia and the European Union, Moldova maintains diplomatic ties with other countries and international organizations, including the United States, China, NATO, and the United Nations. Moldova participates in various multilateral forums and initiatives aimed at promoting regional cooperation, security, and development in Eastern Europe and beyond.

Moldova's international relations are shaped by a complex interplay of geopolitical, economic, and historical factors, as the country seeks to balance its interests and navigate the competing influences of East and West. Despite the challenges and complexities, Moldova remains committed to fostering peaceful and constructive relations with its neighbors and partners, advancing its national interests, and contributing to regional stability and cooperation.

Sustainable Development in Moldova: Preserving Nature and Heritage

Welcome to the chapter on sustainable development in Moldova, a narrative of conservation, preservation, and progress as the country strives to balance economic growth with environmental protection and cultural heritage. Moldova, though a small nation, is rich in natural resources, biodiversity, and historical landmarks, making sustainable development a crucial endeavor for its present and future.

In recent years, Moldova has made significant strides in promoting sustainable development across various sectors, including agriculture, energy, transportation, and tourism. The government has implemented policies and initiatives aimed at fostering environmental sustainability, reducing carbon emissions, and promoting renewable energy sources.

Agriculture plays a vital role in Moldova's economy, but unsustainable agricultural practices can lead to soil degradation, deforestation, and loss of biodiversity. To address these challenges, Moldova has adopted sustainable agricultural practices, including organic farming, crop rotation, and agroforestry, to minimize environmental impact and preserve soil fertility.

In the energy sector, Moldova has prioritized the development of renewable energy sources, such as hydropower, wind power, and solar energy, to reduce dependence on fossil fuels and mitigate greenhouse gas emissions. The country has invested in renewable energy infrastructure and incentivized renewable energy projects through regulatory frameworks and financial support.

Transportation is another area where Moldova is promoting sustainability, with efforts to improve public transportation systems, expand cycling infrastructure, and reduce air pollution from vehicle emissions. The government has implemented policies to encourage the use of electric vehicles and alternative fuels, as well as initiatives to reduce traffic congestion and promote eco-friendly modes of transportation.

Tourism plays a significant role in Moldova's sustainable development strategy, as the country boasts a wealth of cultural heritage sites, natural landscapes, and ecotourism destinations. Moldova has invested in the preservation and promotion of its cultural and natural heritage, including historic landmarks, national parks, and biosphere reserves, to attract eco-conscious tourists and foster sustainable tourism practices.

Furthermore, Moldova is actively engaged in international efforts to promote sustainable development, including the United Nations Sustainable Development Goals (SDGs) and the Paris Agreement on climate change. The country collaborates with international organizations, NGOs, and other stakeholders to exchange best practices, share knowledge, and mobilize resources for sustainable development projects and initiatives.

While Moldova faces numerous challenges on its path to sustainable development, including limited resources, capacity constraints, and external pressures, the country remains committed to its goals of preserving nature and heritage for future generations. Through innovation, collaboration, and a shared commitment to sustainability, Moldova is working to build a more resilient, prosperous, and environmentally conscious society.

Moldova's Transportation Network: Connecting Regions and Beyond

Welcome to the chapter on Moldova's transportation network, a web of roads, railways, waterways, and air routes that connect the country's regions and facilitate movement both domestically and internationally. Moldova's transportation infrastructure plays a vital role in supporting economic development, trade, tourism, and connectivity with neighboring countries and beyond.

The road network is the backbone of Moldova's transportation system, with highways, national roads, and local roads crisscrossing the country's diverse landscapes. The road network connects major cities, towns, and villages, providing access to markets, services, and employment opportunities for residents across the country.

Moldova's railway network complements its road infrastructure, offering an efficient and cost-effective means of transporting goods and passengers. The railway system connects major cities and industrial centers, as well as providing international rail links to neighboring countries such as Romania and Ukraine. Moldova's railway network is operated by Moldovan

Railways (CFM), which manages both passenger and freight services.

In addition to roads and railways, Moldova's waterways play a significant role in transportation, particularly for bulk cargo and agricultural products. The Prut River, which forms part of Moldova's border with Romania, is navigable for small vessels and barges during certain periods of the year, facilitating trade and transport between Moldova and its neighboring countries.

Moldova's air transportation infrastructure is centered around Chisinau International Airport, the country's main airport located near the capital city of Chisinau. Chisinau International Airport serves as the primary gateway for international flights to and from Moldova, connecting the country to major European cities and destinations. The airport handles both passenger and cargo traffic, supporting tourism, trade, and business travel.

In recent years, Moldova has invested in modernizing and upgrading its transportation infrastructure to improve efficiency, safety, and connectivity. The government has implemented infrastructure projects, such as road construction and rehabilitation, railway modernization, and airport expansion, with support from international donors and financial institutions.

Furthermore, Moldova is actively engaged in regional and international transportation initiatives aimed at enhancing connectivity and promoting cross-border cooperation. The country participates in various transport corridors and agreements, such as the European Union's Transport Corridor VII and the Central European Initiative (CEI), to facilitate trade, transit, and mobility within the region.

Despite these efforts, Moldova's transportation network still faces challenges, including inadequate infrastructure, limited funding, and regulatory barriers. The country continues to work towards addressing these challenges and improving its transportation system to meet the needs of its citizens, businesses, and visitors, while also enhancing connectivity and integration with the wider European and global transportation networks.

Exploring Moldova's Rural Life: Homestays and Agritourism

Welcome to the chapter on exploring Moldova's rural life, where the charm of countryside living beckons travelers seeking authentic experiences amidst picturesque landscapes and traditional communities. Moldova's rural areas offer a glimpse into the country's rich agricultural heritage, warm hospitality, and timeless traditions, making them ideal destinations for homestays and agritourism adventures.

In Moldova's rural villages and countryside, visitors can escape the hustle and bustle of city life and immerse themselves in the tranquil beauty of nature. Rolling hills, fertile farmland, and vineyard-dotted valleys characterize the rural landscape, providing a serene backdrop for leisurely strolls, cycling excursions, and outdoor activities.

One of the highlights of exploring rural Moldova is the opportunity to stay in traditional guesthouses and family-run homestays, where guests can experience the warmth and hospitality of local hosts. Homestays offer a unique cultural exchange, allowing visitors to learn about traditional customs, cuisine, and daily life firsthand from their hosts.

Agritourism is another popular activity in rural Moldova, offering visitors the chance to experience the agricultural traditions and practices of the countryside. Visitors can participate in farm activities such as grape harvesting, wine making, fruit picking, and cheese making, gaining insight into the agricultural techniques and processes that sustain rural livelihoods.

Moldova's rural communities take pride in preserving and celebrating their cultural heritage through traditional festivals, events, and rituals. Visitors can experience the vibrant festivities of rural life, from harvest festivals and folk music concerts to seasonal celebrations and religious ceremonies, providing a glimpse into the rich tapestry of Moldovan culture.

Exploring rural Moldova also offers opportunities to taste the flavors of the countryside, with farm-to-table dining experiences showcasing fresh, locally sourced ingredients and traditional recipes. Visitors can savor homemade dishes such as mamaliga (cornmeal porridge), placinta (stuffed pastry), sarmale (stuffed cabbage rolls), and locally produced wines, cheeses, and brandies.

Beyond its natural beauty and cultural treasures, rural Moldova is a haven for outdoor enthusiasts, with scenic hiking trails, birdwatching spots, and eco-tourism destinations waiting to be discovered. From exploring ancient monasteries and archaeological sites to wandering through lush orchards and vineyards, there's no shortage of adventures to be had in rural Moldova.

Overall, exploring Moldova's rural life offers travelers a chance to connect with nature, immerse themselves in local culture, and experience the warmth and hospitality of rural communities. Whether it's a leisurely weekend getaway or an extended agritourism adventure, Moldova's countryside beckons with its timeless charm and authentic experiences.

Moldova's Future: Opportunities and Challenges Ahead

Welcome to the chapter on Moldova's future, where we explore the opportunities and challenges that lie ahead for this small but resilient nation. Moldova, like many countries, faces a complex array of factors that will shape its trajectory in the years to come, ranging from economic opportunities to geopolitical challenges and environmental sustainability.

One of the key opportunities for Moldova's future lies in its strategic location at the crossroads of Europe and Asia. As a landlocked country nestled between Romania and Ukraine, Moldova has the potential to serve as a bridge for trade, investment, and cultural exchange between East and West. With the right policies and infrastructure investments, Moldova can leverage its geographic position to attract foreign investment, expand its export markets, and strengthen its ties with neighboring countries and beyond.

Economic diversification is another important opportunity for Moldova's future development. While agriculture has traditionally been a cornerstone of the Moldovan economy, there is potential for growth in other sectors such as manufacturing, information technology, and tourism. By fostering innovation, entrepreneurship, and skills development, Moldova can capitalize on emerging industries and create new opportunities for job creation and economic prosperity.

Furthermore, Moldova's future hinges on its ability to address pressing social and demographic challenges, including poverty, inequality, and emigration. The country's young and educated workforce represents a valuable asset for economic growth and development, but efforts are needed to retain talent, improve living standards, and provide opportunities for upward mobility. Investing in education, healthcare, and social welfare programs can help ensure that all Moldovans have access to the resources and support they need to thrive in the future.

However, Moldova also faces significant challenges on its path forward, including political instability, corruption, and geopolitical tensions. The country's protracted conflict with the breakaway region of Transnistria, as well as its geopolitical position between Russia and the European Union, present ongoing challenges for governance, security, and national unity. Resolving these issues will require dialogue, compromise, and cooperation both domestically and internationally.

Environmental sustainability is another critical challenge for Moldova's future, as the country grapples with issues such as deforestation, soil erosion, and pollution. Climate change poses additional risks to Moldova's agriculture, water resources, and infrastructure, highlighting the need for proactive measures to mitigate its impacts and build resilience to environmental shocks.

In conclusion, Moldova's future is filled with both opportunities and challenges that will shape the country's development in the years to come. By harnessing its strengths, addressing its weaknesses, and embracing a vision of sustainable, inclusive growth, Moldova can build a brighter future for its citizens and contribute to a more prosperous and peaceful world.

Epilogue

Welcome to the epilogue, the final chapter of our journey through the diverse landscapes, rich history, and vibrant culture of Moldova. As we reflect on the pages of this book, we come away with a deeper understanding of this small but remarkable country and its people.

Moldova, with its rolling hills, fertile plains, and winding rivers, captivates visitors with its natural beauty and tranquility. From the sun-drenched vineyards of its wine-growing regions to the lush forests of its national parks, Moldova's landscapes offer a haven for outdoor enthusiasts and nature lovers alike.

But Moldova's allure goes beyond its scenic beauty. It is a land steeped in history, with ancient fortresses, medieval monasteries, and archaeological sites bearing witness to its rich and complex past. From its origins as a crossroads of civilizations to its struggles for independence and sovereignty, Moldova's history is a tapestry of resilience, perseverance, and cultural diversity.

At the heart of Moldova's identity are its people, whose warmth, hospitality, and spirit of resilience shine through in every aspect of life. Moldovans take pride in their traditions, customs, and cultural heritage, celebrating their unique identity through festivals, music, dance, and cuisine.

As we bid farewell to Moldova, we are reminded of the challenges and opportunities that lie ahead for this young nation. Moldova's future is shaped by its aspirations for economic prosperity, political stability, and social cohesion. It is a future that holds promise for innovation, growth, and development, but also one that requires concerted efforts to address pressing issues such as poverty, corruption, and environmental sustainability.

As travelers, scholars, and adventurers, we leave Moldova with a sense of gratitude for the experiences shared and the memories created. Our journey may end here, but the story of Moldova continues to unfold, inviting new chapters of discovery, exploration, and understanding.

In the end, Moldova remains a land of contrasts, complexities, and untold stories, a place where the past meets the present, and the future holds endless possibilities. As we turn the final page of this book, let us carry with us the lessons learned, the memories cherished, and the hope for a brighter tomorrow for Moldova and its people.